#movements

#WomensMarch

Insisting on Equality

Rebecca Felix

Abdo & Daughters

An Imprint of Abdo Publishing
abdobooks.com

abdobooks.com

Published by Abdo Publishing, a division of ABDO, PO Box 398166, Minneapolis, Minnesota 55439. Copyright © 2020 by Abdo Consulting Group, Inc. International copyrights reserved in all countries. No part of this book may be reproduced in any form without written permission from the publisher. Abdo & Daughters™ is a trademark and logo of Abdo Publishing.

Printed in the United States of America, North Mankato, Minnesota
052019
092019

THIS BOOK CONTAINS
RECYCLED MATERIALS

Design: Aruna Rangarajan, Mighty Media, Inc.
Production: Mighty Media, Inc.
Editor: Liz Salzmann
Cover Photographs: Shutterstock
Interior Photographs: Design elements, Shutterstock; AP Images, pp. 14–15,
    17; Getty Images, pp. 9, 13; Shutterstock, pp. 3, 5, 6–7, 10–11, 19, 21, 22, 25,
    27, 28 (top), 28 (bottom), 29 (top), 29 (bottom)

Library of Congress Control Number: 2018966467

Publisher's Cataloging-in-Publication Data
Names: Felix, Rebecca, author.
Title: #WomensMarch: insisting on equality / by Rebecca Felix
Other title: Insisting on equality
Description: Minneapolis, Minnesota : Abdo Publishing, 2020 | Series:
    #Movements | Includes online resources and index.
Identifiers: ISBN 9781532119347 (lib. bdg.) | ISBN 9781532173806 (ebook)
Subjects: LCSH: Women's rights--United States--Juvenile literature. |
    Equality--United States--Juvenile literature. | Sexism--United States--
    Juvenile literature. | Protest movements--Juvenile literature.
Classification: DDC 305.4--dc2

CONTENTS

It was January 21, 2017. The day before, Donald Trump had been sworn in as president of the United States. Millions of people in the US and around the world rallied together. Many wore pink. They held signs, sang, shouted, and gave speeches. They were advocating for civil rights, women's rights, and reproductive rights.

Social media was the main force behind this global crowd. The idea for a protest grew from a Facebook post by retired lawyer Teresa Shook of Hawaii. She was one of many Americans upset that Trump had been elected president in November 2016. Many people felt Trump did not support equality for women and minorities. They worried these groups' rights were in danger.

On November 8, 2016, Shook posted on Facebook that a pro-women march was needed. Within two days, more than 10,000 social media users had agreed and posted their interest in marching. By January 21, 2017, this number had grown to an estimated 5 million people worldwide.

LET'S TALK TERMS

Women's rights provide women with equal positions of power to men both legally and socially. Reproductive rights give women access to reproductive health services and allow women to make decisions about having children, using birth control, and terminating a pregnancy.

The 2017 Women's March was the largest protest in US history.

The immense number of participants made the Women's March unlike any other event in history. But it was far from the first of its kind. American women have experienced and protested different forms of inequality since the nation was founded.

One of the first issues women worked for was voting rights. For more than one hundred years, women were not allowed to vote in US elections. They were expected to focus on home and family and not get involved in business or politics.

In 1913, more than 5,000 women marched for women's suffrage. They gathered in Washington, DC, the day before President Woodrow Wilson took office. The marchers advocated for Wilson to give them the right to vote.

During the event, onlookers harassed and even assaulted female marchers. The general public became angry when learning of this abuse. This outrage helped form support for the women's suffrage movement.

Advocates supported the movement through protests over the next six years. In 1919, Congress passed the Nineteenth Amendment to the US Constitution. This amendment granted women the right to vote. The amendment was ratified the next year.

The 1913 Women's Suffrage Parade featured nine bands and 20 floats. All were led by an activist riding a white horse.

However, women still had fewer rights than men. So, over the next century, women fought for and earned many of these rights. These included the right to own property and open bank accounts. And they included reproductive rights, such as the right to use birth control and terminate pregnancies. Women also earned the right to take legal action against sexual harassment and assault.

Several protests in Washington, DC, helped women gain support as they fought for these rights. The Rally for Women's Lives was held in 1995. More than 200,000 protestors marched to end violence against women. In 2004, more than one million people joined the March for Women's Lives. This event advocated for protection of women's reproductive rights. Both protests included women and men.

Decades of protests and millions of participants had helped women's rights advocates build support and change laws. But inequalities persisted. Women were still often facing discrimination in the workforce and beyond. And men still held the majority of leadership positions in government.

While many political leaders have supported the fight for women's rights, others have taken positions against the effort. For example, some lawmakers do not believe women should have access to birth control or the right to end a pregnancy. Activists fear that such beliefs threaten the rights women have fought for and earned. And for many, this fear was awoken or intensified during the 2016 presidential campaign.

In 2004, activists at the March for Women's Lives marched outside the White House in defense of women's rights.

Campaign Catalyst

In April 2015, Hillary Rodham Clinton announced that she would run for president of the United States. Many women's rights advocates hoped Clinton would become the first female US president. They believed a female president could help improve gender equality in the nation.

Donald Trump was Clinton's main opponent in the presidential race. Many people felt his running for president was controversial. This was due in large part to his attitude toward women and minorities. During the presidential campaign, Trump made derogatory remarks about these groups.

In October 2016, an audio recording of such remarks increased the controversy surrounding Trump. The tape was made during a 2005 conversation that Trump did not know was being recorded. In the recording, Trump made vulgar comments about women.

When the recording was released, many Americans were shocked and disgusted by Trump's comments. In spite of this reaction, Trump was elected president. Trump's supporters felt he would bring positive change to the government. But others feared Trump would threaten civil rights, women's rights, and reproductive rights. People shared these fears on social media.

Teresa Shook was one of these people. On the evening of November 8, she created a Facebook event calling for a pro-women march in reaction to Trump's win. By the next morning, 10,000 people had replied that they were interested in attending the march!

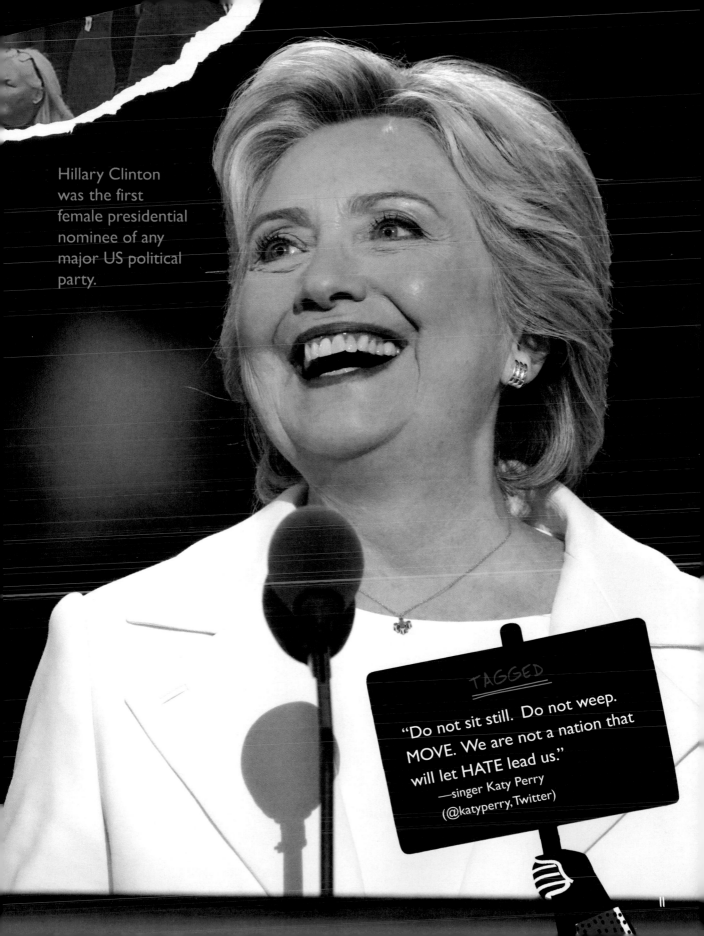

Hillary Clinton was the first female presidential nominee of any major US political party.

TAGGED

"Do not sit still. Do not weep. MOVE. We are not a nation that will let HATE lead us."
—singer Katy Perry
(@katyperry, Twitter)

11

As Shook's idea for a pro-women march spread, organizers and leaders sprang into action. Bob Bland, a female fashion entrepreneur in New York City, had an idea similar to Shook's. Bland contacted Shook and suggested they join forces to create a large march that included people from throughout the US.

Bland got additional activists and organizers involved. These included gun control advocate Tamika D. Mallory, criminal justice reform advocate Carmen Perez, and activist Linda Sarsour. Shook remained involved in the event but let these experienced activists take over leadership.

The organizers named the event the Women's March on Washington and decided to hold it on January 21, 2017. This was to be Trump's first full day as president of the United States. The main march would take place in Washington, DC. Sister marches were planned in cities across the nation and around the world. Each sister march had its own leaders who worked with the Washington march leaders. This helped keep the events organized.

Women's March organizers relied heavily on social media to organize the event. Facebook, Twitter, and Instagram made it easy for participants to join the movement and find information about the marches. These sites also provided Women's March leaders with a platform to communicate the march's message.

"I didn't have a plan or a thought about what would happen," Shook said of her Facebook post. "I just kept saying, I think we should march."

FACES OF #WOMENSMARCH

Bob Bland is a fashion designer and advocate for sustainable, ethical supply chains. She is the CEO and founder of Manufacture New York. This organization develops new ideas for designing and producing clothing and fabric.

Linda Sarsour is a former executive director of the Arab American Association of New York. She has led or organized several protests on issues such as police brutality, immigration reform, and criminal justice reform.

Carmen Perez

is executive director of national human and civil rights organization The Gathering for Justice. She has organized many national events and is an expert in juvenile and criminal justice.

Tamika D. Mallory

is an advocate for women's rights, healthcare reform, and gun control. She was the youngest executive director of the civil rights organization National Action Network.

"#womensmarch is providing space for every woman who believes in justice, equity and freedom."
— Tamika D. Mallory
(@TamikaDMallory, Twitter)

As more people took interest in the march, its organizers became busier. Many slept only a few hours a night. They were on social media almost constantly, spreading information about the event, communicating with other organizers, and sharing the event's mission.

Trump's election led to the idea for the march. Because of this, the public largely viewed the event as an anti-Trump protest. However, march organizers insisted the event was not anti-Trump but pro-women. The event's official mission was to "harness the political power of diverse women and their communities to create transformative social change."

The event's focus spread beyond women's rights, however. It also supported reproductive rights, LGBTQIA rights, worker's rights, civil rights, disability rights, immigrant rights, and environmental protection. Women's March leaders hoped to demonstrate that people from different backgrounds can unite under shared goals. As the day of the march approached, people around the world did just that.

WHY DO PEOPLE MARCH?

March organizers feel this type of protest sends a powerful message. Marches earn the attention of the public, media, and people in power. Marching together also creates solidarity. It shows that there are many others who support the same cause. Finally, marches create tension. They can be loud and energetic. March organizers hope this energy inspires people to take further action for change.

I AM HERE FOR MY GRANDMOTHER MOTHER & DAUGHTERS ! I AM HERE FOR ALL WOMEN!

Men were encouraged to participate in the Women's March. Many men marched to support the women and girls in their lives.

It's Girls Like
be will one day

17

Women's March participants included people of all genders, races, religions, and sexual orientations. Many prepared for the event by connecting with fellow marchers on social media. Celebrities also got involved, encouraging their fans to join the cause. As the event neared, friends, families, and colleagues planned trips to march together in Washington, DC, or at sister marches.

People also gathered to make protest signs to carry during the march. Many even made or bought matching clothing to create a unified look or express a certain message. The most prominent piece of clothing was a special pink hat.

These pink hats had two points on them to resemble cat ears. This represented a slang term for *cat*. The slang term is also used to refer to a woman's private parts. Trump used the term in the 2005 audio recording in which he made vulgar comments about women. Outrage over his use of this term inspired the pink hats.

Pink hat makers and wearers wanted to send a message to Trump and others who use this term in a derogatory way. The protestors wanted to express that they would not be oppressed by the term. Instead, they would use it as a symbol of joining together and fighting back. The pink cat-ear hats became an unofficial Women's March uniform.

The first pink hat pattern was designed by Kat Coyle, a yarn shop owner in Los Angeles, California. She put the pattern online so people all over the world could knit their own hats.

It's Girls Like N

In the days leading up to the march, people from around the world flooded Washington, DC. The event's organizers expected about 200,000 people to attend the main march. But about 500,000 people showed up!

Sister marches took place in all 50 US states and in more than 30 countries. There was even a march in Antarctica! The *Washington Post* estimated that 4.1 million people took part in US marches. And about 300,000 people in other countries marched that day. The location with the most attendees was Los Angeles, California. There, the crowd size was estimated at about 750,000 people.

A majority of marchers across all locations held signs with words of either protest or inspiration. Many of these signs addressed the topic of women's rights. But signs also shared messages supporting reproductive rights, environmental protection, immigrant rights, and more.

TAGGED

"Thanks for standing, speaking & marching for our values @womensmarch. Important as ever. I truly believe we're always Stronger Together."
—Hillary Clinton
(@HillaryClinton, Twitter)

Marchers in Washington, DC, walked from the Capitol to the White House. There were so many people that it was sometimes hard to move in the large crowd.

Protesters also used social media to speak out on the day of the march. About 337,000 Instagram posts were tagged with #WomensMarch and related hashtags that day. Facebook and Twitter were also flooded with march-related posts on January 21. Users posted photos and video clips of marchers, words of inspiration and empowerment, and reactions to the massive crowds. But in some locations, the crowds were so large that using social media was impossible.

In Washington, DC, so many protestors tried to access their Twitter, Facebook, or Instagram apps that local networks crashed! Many protesters had to wait until after the march to share their images. This sharing continued for days following the march. On January 24, Instagram users were still posting more than 300 Women's March photos an hour!

TAGGED

"Today…we march for our rights. Not just as women, but as human beings. We are entitled to equal rights like GENDER EQUALITY, EDUCATION, EQUAL PAY, REPRODUCTIVE RIGHTS, FREEDOM FROM SEXUAL ASSAULTS… because womens rights are human rights."
—singer Demi Lovato
(@ddlovato, Instagram)

Activists of all ages joined the Women's March.

The hashtag #WomensMarch helped organize one of the largest protests in world history. But to Women's March organizers, the march was more than a one-day event. It was the beginning of a movement inspiring people to stand up together and fight oppression.

The Women's March was an example of how solidarity empowers others to stand up and speak out. In the year following the event, march leaders worked to keep this movement alive. They arranged smaller protests around the US and encouraged women to vote and run for political office. This led to an increase in the number of women running for office across the nation. The march also encouraged leaders already working in politics to push for positive changes and bills to support women's rights.

The Women's March was followed by another hashtag movement related to women's rights. In October 2017, the *New York Times* published a story about the sexual harassment and assault that women in Hollywood have experienced. Actress Alyssa Milano posted about this story on Twitter. This led to the hashtag #MeToo, which encourages people to stand together against sexual harassment and abuse. The hashtag went viral and strengthened a growing movement of female empowerment across the nation and world.

On the one-year anniversary of posting her tweet, Milano said, "The most beautiful thing from all of this is not only women standing up and using their voices but standing up for each other in solidarity."

25

A Growing Movement

The Women's March grew from an event into a movement. It encouraged people to band together and speak out on many issues. The Women's March came to stand for a unified group fighting for gender equality and social justice.

On January 20, 2018, a second Women's March was held in cities across the US. This march was also in support of women's rights and reproductive rights. But this time, it focused on encouraging people to vote in support of these and other issues. The crowds at the 2018 marches weren't as massive as the previous year's. However, an estimated 1.6 to 2.5 million people participated. A third march, called #WomensWave, occurred on January 19, 2019.

Years after its first event, the Women's March movement continues to grow. Women, minorities, and other oppressed groups rose up and joined forces on a winter day in 2017. They and their supporters have remained standing together ever since.

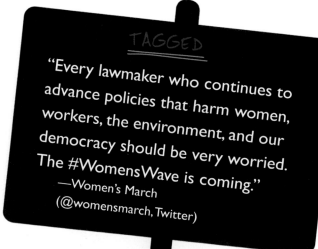

TAGGED

"Every lawmaker who continues to advance policies that harm women, workers, the environment, and our democracy should be very worried. The #WomensWave is coming."
—Women's March
(@womensmarch, Twitter)

The second Women's March was not only a protest. In many cities, attendees could also register to vote.

TIMELINE

The Nineteenth Amendment is ratified, allowing women in the US to vote.

The March for Women's Lives takes place in Washington, DC, advocating for protection of reproductive rights.

A 2005 audio recording of US presidential candidate Donald Trump is released. On the recording, Trump makes vulgar comments about women.

1920

2004

October 2016

1913

1995

November 2016

The Rally for Women's Lives takes place in Washington, DC, to protest violence against women.

More than 5,000 women march to protest that their gender is denied the right to vote.

Trump is elected US president. Hawaii resident Teresa Shook suggests on Facebook that a pro-women march be organized in response to the election. Her suggestion goes viral.

Official Program
WOMAN SUFFRAGE
Procession

Washington D.C.
March 3, 1913

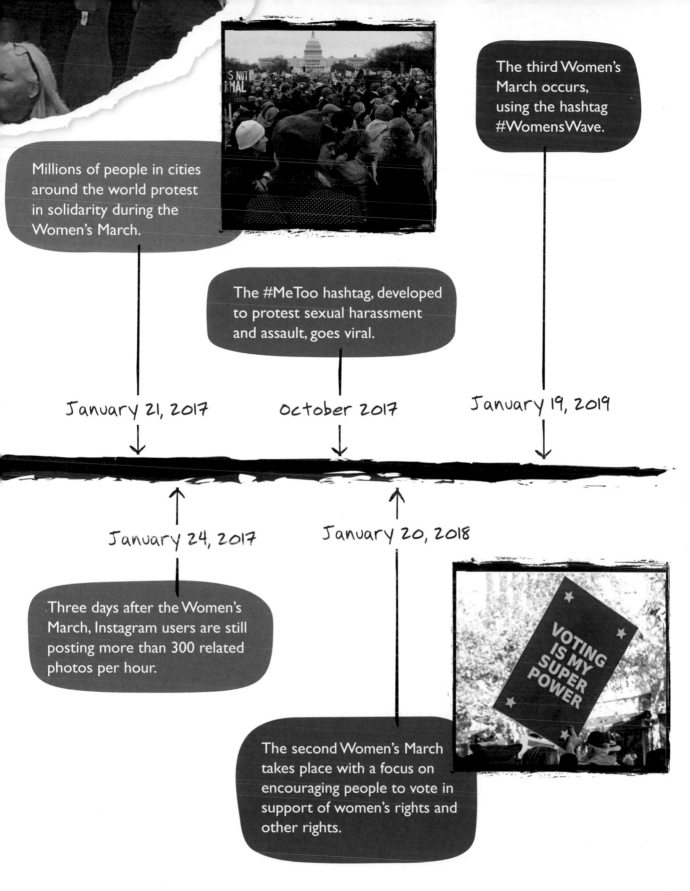

Millions of people in cities around the world protest in solidarity during the Women's March.

The #MeToo hashtag, developed to protest sexual harassment and assault, goes viral.

The third Women's March occurs, using the hashtag #WomensWave.

January 21, 2017

October 2017

January 19, 2019

January 24, 2017

January 20, 2018

Three days after the Women's March, Instagram users are still posting more than 300 related photos per hour.

VOTING IS MY SUPER POWER

The second Women's March takes place with a focus on encouraging people to vote in support of women's rights and other rights.

GLOSSARY

activist—a person who takes direct action in support of or in opposition to an issue that causes disagreement.

advocate—to defend or support a cause. An advocate is a person who defends or supports a cause.

amendment—a change to a country's or a state's constitution.

audio—of or relating to the sound that is heard on a recording or broadcast.

colleague—someone who works with others in a certain field, at a job, or on a particular project.

derogatory—showing a lack of respect for someone or something.

discrimination—unfair treatment, often based on race, religion, or gender.

diverse—made up of people who are different from one another.

empower—to help people gain control over their own lives. This process is called empowerment.

entrepreneur—one who organizes, manages, and accepts the risks of a business or an enterprise.

gender—the behaviors, characteristics, and qualities most often associated with either the male or female sex.

harass—to annoy or bother someone again and again. This behavior is called harassment.

hashtag—a word or phrase used in social media posts, such as tweets, that starts with the symbol # and that briefly indicates what the post is about.

participate—to take part or share in something. Someone who participates is a participant.

pregnancy—the condition of having one or more babies growing within the body.

social media—websites or smartphone apps that provide information and entertainment and allow people to communicate with each other. Facebook and Twitter are examples of social media.

solidarity—a feeling of unity between people who have the same interests, goals, or experiences.

suffrage—the right to vote.

transformative—causing important and lasting change.

viral—quickly or widely spread, usually by electronic communication.

vulgar—very rude or impolite.

ONLINE RESOURCES

Booklinks
NONFICTION NETWORK
FREE! ONLINE NONFICTION RESOURCES

To learn more about #WomensMarch, please visit **abdobooklinks.com** or scan this QR code. These links are routinely monitored and updated to provide the most current information available.

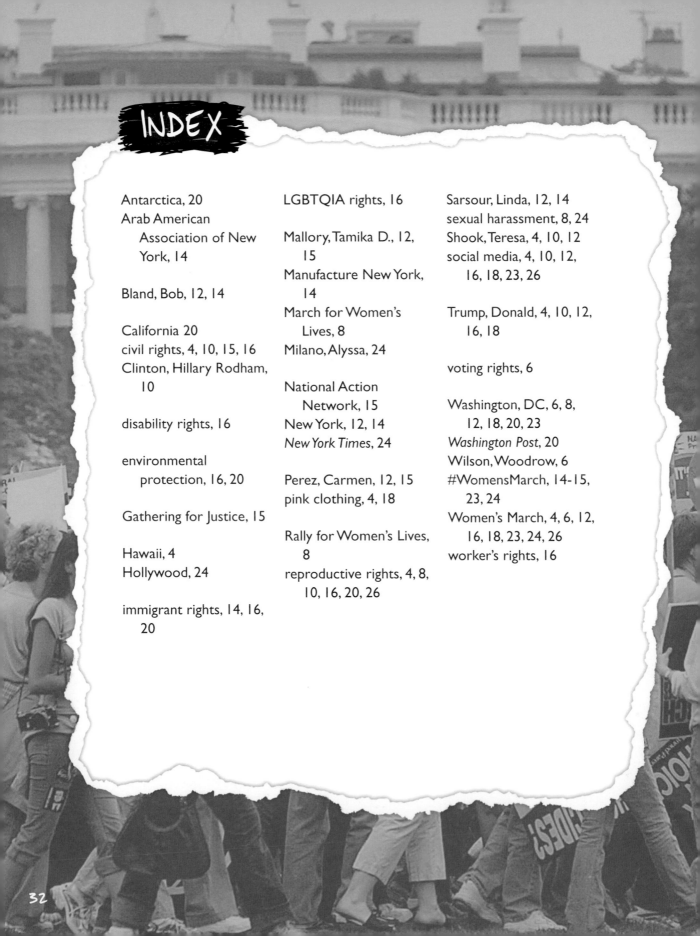

INDEX